THE POWER OF METAPHYSICS

A 27-Day Journey To A New Life

TABLE OF CONTENTS

INTRODUCTION 5

WEEK 1 ∧ THE SILENT DISCOVERY: WHY SILENCE IS THE GREATEST TEACHING 8

DAY 1 CHALLENGING PERCEPTION 10

DAY 2 THE NATURE OF THE MIND 15

DAY 3 PERCEIVING THE ILLUSIONS OF REALITY 21

DAY 4 PHENOMENAL VS. NON-PHENOMENAL 26

DAY 5 MEDITATION 30

DAY 6 THE NATURE OF EXPERIENCE 34

DAY 7 THE PSYCHOLOGICAL SELF 39

WEEK 2 Γ THE POWER OF THOUGHTS AND BELIEFS: HOW THE MIND CREATES REALITY 45

DAY 8 VALUES 50

DAY 9 BELIEFS 53

DAY 10 ACCESSING YOUR BELIEFS 54

DAY 11 CHANGING A BELIEF 56

DAY 12 PREPARING FOR CHANGE 59

DAY 13 & 14 ACCEPTANCE AND RESISTANCE 60

WEEK 3 Θ FOCUS: THE MIND'S SWORD FOR CUTTING THROUGH OBSTACLES 63

DAY 15 PROBLEM SOLVING 66

DAY 16 MANIFESTATION 70

DAY 17 & 18 VISUALIZATIONS 71

DAY 19 CHANGING PERCEPTION 73

WEEK 4 Φ FEELINGS AND EMOTIONS: MESSENGERS FROM THE UNIVERSE 75

DAY 20 OBSERVING SENSATIONS 77

DAY 21 OBSERVING EMOTIONS 79

DAY 22 TRANSFORMING SENSATIONS 82

DAY 23 EXPERIENCE FREEDOM 84

DAY 24 TRUST YOUR FEELINGS 86

DAY 25 TRANSFORMING EMOTIONS 89

DAY 26 LETTING GO 92

DAY 27 Ω CHALLENGING MINDS AND CULTIVATING FREEDOM 95

3

© **Copyright 2017 - All rights reserved.**

The contents of this book may not be reproduced, duplicated or transmitted without direct written permission from the author.

Under no circumstances will any legal responsibility or blame be held against the publisher for any reparation, damages, or monetary loss due to the information herein, either directly or indirectly.

Legal Notice:

This book is copyright protected. This is only for personal use. You cannot amend, distribute, sell, use, quote or paraphrase any part or the content within this book without the consent of the author.

Disclaimer Notice:

Please note the information contained within this document is for educational and entertainment purposes only. Every attempt has been made to provide accurate, up to date and reliable complete information. No warranties of any kind are expressed or implied. Readers acknowledge that the author is not engaging in the rendering of legal, financial, medical or professional advice. The content of this book has been derived from various sources. Please consult a licensed professional before attempting any techniques outlined in this book.

By reading this document, the reader agrees that under no circumstances are is the author responsible for any losses, direct or indirect, which are incurred as a result of the use of information contained within this document, including, but not limited to, —errors, omissions, or inaccuracies.

Introduction

In an old parable, a wise old farmer stepped outside of his home to take in the evening air. Looking out toward the horizon, he gazed at a magnificent moon. As he admired the moon, his grandson came out to join him. The two chatted for a while when his grandson asked him the following question. "Grandpa, what is the secret to becoming happy?" The farmer whistled for his dog to come, which ran right over. The farmer pointed his finger at the moon. In reaction to the farmer's gesture, the dog fixated his gaze on the farmer's finger.

The farmer turned to his grandson and replied: "I was pointing to a magnificent moon, but my dog placed its focus on my finger." Most of us behave like the dog in the parable. We have placed our focus on what we believe points to happiness rather than experiencing happiness as it naturally exists.

There has never been a person who has not sought happiness. We may not be consciously seeking happiness; however, we are doing so subconsciously. The pursuit of happiness is hardwired within us. Even a person who takes their own life does so because they feel that it would be less painful than living. To borrow from a famous song, we are looking for happiness in all the wrong places.

Just as the farmer's dog, we are fixated on finding happiness by focusing on objects while being unaware of its source. What are the objects that we focus on in our pursuit of happiness? The list is endless. The more popular ones are relationships, sex, money, our careers, status, power, alcohol, drugs, the approval of others, and so on. In fact, anything that you can think, see, hear, touch, or taste, is an object and can become the object of our focus. Anything that you can conceptualize in your mind or detect with your senses is considered phenomenal. Since we experience the world phenomenally, this is where most of us have sought out our happiness.

True happiness and freedom occur when we shift our attention from that which seems to point to happiness and start focusing the nature of happiness itself. In order focus on the nature of happiness, we first need focus on the nature of who we are. It is by taking on the endless journey into the self that all that we could desire is revealed to us.

This book is about learning to shift your perspective. It is by shifting your perspective from the world of objects to the nature of awareness that you will be able to partake in the endless journey into the self. To assist you in this journey, this book is divided into five chapters, with each chapter dedicated to a specific core principle in metaphysics. In turn, each chapter represents a week of practices that you can easily apply in your daily life.

By the end of this book, you will have developed a basic foundation for changing the trajectory of your life. Are you ready to stop focusing on the pointers in our life and start to gazing at the magnificent moon that is your truth?

Week 1
ʌ
The Silent Discovery: Why Silence is the greatest Teaching

Imagine that you are walking into a forest, and you come across a small pond. You throw a small rock into the pond and then look into it. Your reflection in its waters is distorted by the ripples from the splash. After a few minutes, the ripples disappear and leave the water surface as smooth as glass. This time when you look into the pond you see a clear image of yourself. Not only do you see a clear image of yourself, you see a clear image of everything around you, the trees, the mountains, and the sky.

For most of us, our experience of life is like the pond with ripples. We never clearly see into the nature of life, or of ourselves, because of the distortion that we experience. The distortion I speak of are the ripples of illusions that are created when lack clarity in how we perceive our essential nature.

We have clarity of our essential nature because we have lost the silence within us, the silence which is our direct connection with the essence of who we are. The good news is that the silence that I speak of never was lost, to lose it is impossible. Rather, we have forgotten about it due to our fixation on objects.

We have forgotten about silence because we have been socialized to experience life as being something outside ourselves. This socialization goes back for innumerable generations. Because we have divorced ourselves from our essential self, we have become fixated with the objects of our lives. We have allowed these objects to define our sense of self and the quality of our lives.

Both silence and objects are inherent aspects of life. In fact, silence is also an object. I will address this point later on in the book. For now, we will discuss the significance of silence. The silence that we will be discovering has nothing to do with any sounds that may be in your environment. The silence that I speak of is the stillness that is within you.

Day 1
~
Challenging Perception

We will start off with a simple exercise that can facilitate the experiencing of silence and the nature of awareness (note: This exercise may take practice before you experience its effect).

1. Sit down, make yourself comfortable.
2. Place your awareness on an object within your environment. I want you to observe this object, making it the point of your focus.
3. If I asked you to report back to me of what you know about the object, what would you tell me?

I would guess that you would tell me the name of the object, a description of what it looks like, and perhaps what the object was doing. For example, if the object that I was looking at was a tree, I could tell you of its appearance, its color, its height, and the shape of its leaves. I may even be able to tell you the species that the tree belongs to and where this species of tree is found.

Now that I have given you my example, take a look at your object again. What is it that you know about your object?

Now that you have finished with this exercise, we are ready to bring our discussion back to silence. If you are like most of humanity, your report back to me would be comprised of facts and opinions about your object. Your report back to me might be stated in one sentence, or you may be able to give an extensive account of your experience. Regardless of what you report back, you will most likely believe the findings of your observation are an accurate account of your object. We will now take the last exercise and break it down to challenge your experience of observing.

1. Look at your object again. How is it that you know the size of your object, its color, or any other information that you see? Most likely, you would reply back "Because I saw it."
2. Take another look at your object. Determine for yourself if you can separate the seeing of the object from the object itself. In other words, can I separate my seeing of the tree from the tree itself? Put another way, is there a point where seeing stops and your object begins or do the act of seeing and your object merge into each other? I hope that you will realize that the act of seeing and the object being seen are inseparable from each other.
3. Assuming that you agree with me that the seeing of your object is dependent on the existence of the object itself, my next question to you is how do you know that seeing is taking place? You know that the act of seeing is taking place because you

are aware of it. You have awareness that seeing is taking place.
4. Now, look at your object again. Can you separate the awareness of the seeing from the act of seeing? This question may be more difficult than the last question, so take your time to determine this for yourself. Eventually, you will realize that the awareness of seeing and the act of seeing are also one in the same.

Let us summarize what we have just discovered:

- The seeing of the object and the object itself are one in the same.
- The awareness of the act of seeing and the act of seeing itself are also one in the same.

We can conclude from these realizations that nothing exists apart from awareness, that awareness and that which is known are inseparable from each other. If you were able to experience that which I was guiding you toward in this exercise, look at your object again from this new perspective. Do you feel differently about your experience of seeing? Does it change what you can tell me about your object?

Before you first did this exercise, your first observation of the object was like the pond that just had the rock thrown into it. Like the ripples of the pond, your thoughts distorted any deeper experience of your object that you could have potentially experienced.

As you practice this exercise, using the guidance that I offered, the ripples that are created by your mind's activities will gradually diminish. Just like the still water of the pond, your experience of life will be clearer, more unified. The previous exercise can also be adjusted to apply to remaining four senses.

Silence, also known as stillness, is the ability not to get caught up in our mind's chatter and to be able to discern the subtleties of reality that reflect its essential nature. You cannot know anything about that which you experience; you can only have a knowing (awareness) of the existence of experience.

I cannot know anything about a tree. I can only know of my perceptions of the tree. I can know of the sensations that I feel when I touch the tree, and I can know of the sounds of its leaves rustling in the wind. I can also know of my thoughts of the tree, but I cannot know the tree itself. When awareness illuminates experience, without being distorted by our thinking, the secrets of the universe will reveal themselves as effortlessly as the reflections of still water. This is the power of silence.

Daily Exercise:

The exercise that you did in this section normally needs to be practiced before you can experience a notable change in how you perceive reality. Continue practice this exercise.

Day 2
~
The Nature of the Mind

There is a story of a servant whose master lived in a large mansion. The strange thing was the relationship that the servant had with his master in that the servant had never seen him! The master never ventured from his room, and all communication occurred through the closed door of the master's bedroom. If the master needed something, he would signal the servant who would come to his closed door to receive his orders.

One day, the servant was telling his friend about his frustration that he was experiencing with his master. He shared with his friend that his master was never satisfied, that he was always finding fault with him. His master was always demanding more from him. His friend suggested that he should discuss his concerns with his master. His friend's advice rang true for him. He needed to tell his master how he felt. Gathering his courage, he went to his master's room and knocked on the door. To his surprise, his master did not respond. He knocked a second time, still no response. The servant began to worry. Could it be that his master was in trouble?

The servant gathered his nerve and reached for the doorknob. To his shock, the door was unlocked! When he opened the door, he was left speechless. The room was empty! There was not master, no furniture, no carpet, no curtains; there was nothing! The servant sunk into despair. He realized that he had spent his life serving a master that did not exist!

The story that you just read is a metaphor for the relationship that most of us have with our minds. The servant symbolizes you and me; the master represents our minds. Just like the servant, most of us live out our lives obeying our minds. Just like the master, our minds are constantly making demands of us and are never satisfied. All problems that we experience, both at the individual and collective level, are the result of our unquestioned allegiance to our minds.

My hope for you is that by applying the core metaphysical principles that are found in this book, you will gradually experience a shift in your relationship with your mind. Instead of your mind being in charge of you, you will take charge of your mind. Instead of a being a tyrant who is always demanding more from you, your mind will serve you as a tool for us solve problems, creating new possibilities, and explore higher levels of consciousness.

In the last section, you performed exercises that invited you to inquire into the subtleties of observing an object. The mind operates at the conceptual level. In other words, the mind can only detect those things that can be discerned by the senses or conceived as a concept by the mind. Those things in our experience that possess these qualities are considered to be phenomenal. That which can be perceived through our senses is registered by the mind. The mind operates by creating conceptual representations of the information that it obtains from our senses. When I look at a tree, my eyes take in visual information about the tree and convert into electric impulses by way of the optic nerve. When the electric impulses reach the brain, it descrambles the digitized information and reassembles it into a conceptual image of the tree.

Whenever we experience anything conceptually, we perceive an image created by the mind, rather than perceiving the truth of its existence. The "tree" that I see in my backyard is not the true reality. The "tree" that I experience is a conceptual image in my mind that I believe is the actual tree. It is for this reason that I made the statement the last section that we can never know anything about our experiences; we can only know of experience. The only thing that I can know about a tree is my knowing of its conceptual image.

Regarding the exercises from the previous section, if you were able to experience how the awareness of an object and the object itself are indivisible, then you had a most profound discovery that eludes the majority of humanity. That fact that most of humanity has not had this experience leads to the understanding why true freedom remains just an idealistic notion for most of us.

The achievement of true freedom is independent of the conditions of our lives. There are people in prison who enjoy greater freedom than some multi-millionaires. The experience of true freedom is the product of mastering our relationship with our minds.

There is not one problem that a human being can experience that is not the result of a limited sense of self. At the deepest level, the root of all actions or behaviors is thought. Everything that we do originates from thought. Essentially, there are only two kinds of thoughts, fearful and loving. Thoughts of fear are based on a sense of separation, that we are separate from the rest of life. Thoughts of love arise from a sense of connection, from a sense of an oneness with life. Sincere, loving thoughts remove our sense of separation, fear does not exist. It is difficult for us not to feel separate from life when most of us experience life through the concepts that we create of it.

Imagine that you go to the Grand Canyon and come across the most amazing scenic view of the canyon's majesty. You witness the beautifully rugged canyon walls, the amazing rock formations, and its raging waters. You are so impressed with what you see that you decide to take a picture of it using a cheap disposable camera. When you look at the developed picture, you realize that it no way does the picture come even close to that which you experienced. Similarly, our concepts are like the photograph. They are a poor representation of the infinite grandeur that is life.

Most of us experience life through our concepts of it. In fact, our sense of self is also a concept. The reason why most of us are servants to our minds is that we believe in the concepts that are our minds create, including our sense of self.

Here is a simple exercise. Answer this question: Who are you? When most people are asked this question, they come up with responses (if they can come up with a response at all) such as:

- I am a man
- I am a woman
- I am undeserving
- I am a good person.
- I am shy.
- I am a rebel.
- I am a parent.
- I am a teacher.
- I am a winner.
- I am a human being.
- I am a citizen of the planet.

Regardless of how you answer this question, you are using concepts to define who you are. We have identified ourselves with concepts because we have personalized our experience of it. We experience ourselves based on what our mind tells us. It is only through silence that we can transcend our concepts and experience for ourselves that aspect of ourselves that is more fundamental than anything that the mind can grasp. To transcend our minds is to change our relationship with it. When we transcend our mind, we become like the servant who found out that his master's room was empty.

Day 3
~
Perceiving the Illusions of Reality

So far in this chapter, we explored inner silence and the nature of the mind. We also discussed how we focus on objects, which make up the phenomenal world. We discussed that the phenomenal world includes everything that we can detect with our minds or senses. Most of us live out our lives from the phenomenal perspective. In other words, our awareness is limited to the world of form.

Because our focus is on the world of form, we have come to identify with the world form. How we define ourselves, how we experience ourselves, is often determined by the phenomenal. Here is an example:

Joe is driving his car to work when he gets cut off by another driver, who is not paying attention. Joe experiences anger and curses the other driver. When he arrives at work, Joe is informed by his boss that he will be getting a bonus. Hearing this news, Joe is happy. Later that day, Joe gets a call from a difficult client. Joe becomes frustrated. At the end of the day, Joe arrives home and is embraced by his family. Now, Joe feels loved and supported.

Through his day, Joe experienced a wide range of emotional states, and each state caused Joe to experience himself differently. Further, he believed that the changes to his emotional state were due to the situations that he encountered. He attributes these changes to the other driver, the bonus, the difficult client, and his family. Joe is an example of how our sense of self is shaped by the situations and events of our lives. Because change is a constant in life, our sense of self is unstable. One moment we can feel like that we are on the top of the world, only to feel defeated when the winds of change blow by us.

Now consider your own life. What has changed in your life since you were a young child? Have your thoughts changed? Have your beliefs changed? Have your relationships changed? Has your body changed? Has your experience of the world changed? Has the way you see yourself changed? Everything that you have ever experienced has changed at some level. Nothing in life remains static or constant, at least at the phenomenal level.

For us to say that everything in life changes; however, it not enough. How do you know change is occurring? You know that change is occurring the same way you knew of the object in the previous exercise. You know of change because you are aware of it. However, for you to be aware of change, you need to be aware of that which does not change. How can you know anything without knowing the opposite? How can you know cold unless you also know hot? How can you know calm unless you also know anger?

There is an aspect of you that is aware of change, including the changes that you undergo physically, mentally, and emotionally. The reason why this aspect of you is aware of change is that it is changeless. Only that which is changeless can perceive that which changes. How else could change be known? There is an aspect of you that exists within the silence of your being and is beyond any concept. The aspect that I speak of cannot be comprehended by the mind, for this non-phenomenal. To say something is non-phenomenal is to say that it cannot be detected by the senses or conceived by the mind.

What we refer to as "reality" is the unfolding of life, an unfolding that is witnessed by your non-phenomenal self. There is no true reality; rather, what we refer to as reality is the constantly changing projection of consciousness. The illusions of reality are that we live in a physical world, of which we are a separate entity. We see ourselves as being separate from other people, other objects, and from our environment. Because we experience ourselves as being separate, we pursue the objects of the physical realm in the belief that they will make us happy and free us from our sufferings.

Because nothing in the phenomenal world is permanent, we experience a sense of loss or disappointment when things change. We are like a hamster on the wheel. No matter how fast we run, we never get to where we want to be, that place where lasting peace exists. We have fallen for the illusions of reality, that there is something out there that will give us what we want to experience.

Ultimate peace comes from establishing ourselves in the unchanging while enjoying the experience of the changing. The unchanging is your essential being. That which changes is the myriad expressions of your essential being. That which you experience as being you is the form that your essential being used to experiences the myriad expressions of itself. It was stated earlier that awareness of experience and experience itself are inseparable. Your essential being is awareness, and all that you are aware of is experience. Because awareness cannot be separate from experience, you are one with all that is.

Daily Exercise:

Here is an exercise for developing your ability to perceive without conceptualizing your experience:

1. Sit down and view your surroundings, taking your time to take everything in.

2. When you are ready, close your eyes and allow yourself to relax.

3. Imagine that you are an alien from a distant planet who has arrived on Earth to study it. You have no information about this planet, nor do you have any past experience to draw from. Because of this, you are unable to define, identify, analyze, or judge anything that you experience. In other words, you are a blank slate.

4. No open your eyes and look at your surroundings again. Take your time.

5. How did your experience observing compare with your first observation?

If you did not notice any difference between the two observations, practice this exercise until you do. Anytime we incorporate our thoughts or judgments while observing, we perceive things conceptually. To be able to observe without utilizing conceptual thinking is part of being mindful and present.

Day 4
~
Phenomenal vs. Non-Phenomenal

In this chapter, there has been frequent reference to the terms phenomenal and non-phenomenal. To quickly review, phenomenal refers to anything that you can experience directly. Everything that we know about our world is phenomenal. Anything that exists beyond our ability to perceive is non-phenomenal. Our minds function conceptually, meaning that information that is received by the mind is converted into a concept.

Words and images are an example of conceptual constructs of the mind. Words and images are solely the product of the mind. Without the mind, images and words would not exist. We do not "see" images. As indicated before, our eyes take in visual information, which is converted to electrical impulses. The electrical impulses are then converted into images by the brain. Similarly, words are linguistic constructions of the mind that are used to convey a thought. You may wonder why I switch from using "mind" to "brain." For now, I am writing this way purely for reasons of semantics. We will discuss later the difference between the mind and the brain.

If images are the products of the information that is gathered by sight, and words are the mind's representation of thought, where does information and thought come from? Thought and information are one in the same. What we call thought is information that is perceived by consciousness. At the most fundamental, everything that exists is information. However, we can go one step further. Information is a form of energy. Everything that exists is an expression of energy. However, this energy is not the kind of energy that we experience in our daily lives. The kind of energy I am speaking of is not electrical. The energy that I speak of is aware of itself. The energy that I am speaking of is consciousness.

In the first section of this book, you did an exercise where you observed an object. In doing this exercise, you hopefully concluded that it is impossible to separate the awareness of an object with the object itself. Awareness and consciousness are just two different terms for the same thing. The fundamental nature of all that exists is consciousness. Everything that exists arises from consciousness. Without consciousness, there can be no experience.

Going back to the terms non-phenomenal and phenomenal, these are just concepts that our mind uses to explain that which it can perceive and that which it cannot. In truth, words, concepts, mind, this book, and you, are just the physical manifestations of consciousness. At the most basic level, there is no difference between the phenomenal realm and a non-phenomenal realm. There is no difference between spirituality and materialism. There is no difference between reality and fantasy. Finally, there is no difference between you and universe itself. Any sense of difference or distinction is a product of our minds.

There are researchers who are spending countless hours pursuing the origins of the universe or the nature of matter. Their searches will be never-ending. They are chasing concepts when the answers that they are looking for lie in the depths of their own lives.

Daily Exercise:

1. Sit down and allow yourself to relax.
2. Now, look at an object that you are familiar with. Make this object the focus of your attention.
3. When you have familiarized yourself with this object, close your eyes and visualize this object in your mind, to the best of your ability.

Every one visualizes differently, so do not make any judgments about your ability to visualize. Imagine your object to the best of your abilities.

4. When you have the image in your mind, notice the qualities of this image. How does this image appear to you? Is it blurry or clear? Is faint without any distinguishable features or does have it vivid detail? Do the qualities of your image

change in intensity or form, or do they remain static?
5. Can you determine where your image appeared from? Can you determine where your image goes when it fades?
6. Now visualize something that is imaginary, something that does not exist in your reality. Perhaps it is a unicorn or a purple elephant.
7. When you have the image in your mind, notice the qualities of this image. How does this image appear to you? Is it blurry or clear? Is faint without any distinguishable features or does have it vivid detail? Do the qualities of your image change in intensity or form, or do they remain static?
8. Can you determine where your image appeared from? Can you determine where your image goes when it fades?

Is there any difference between your visualization of the imaginary object and the one you that you observed? Can you tell the difference between "reality" and "fantasy"?

Day 5
~
Meditation

So far in this first chapter, we have discussed silence, the illusions of the mind, and phenomenal and non-phenomenal existence. Hopefully you have found this discussion interesting; however, everything that you have read so far is just a concept. It has been just food for your mind. Concepts are necessary aspect of being human beings. We are social creatures who need concepts to communicate and exchange ideas. For this purpose, concepts are invaluable.

The same is true of the mind. Our minds are the key to our evolutionary success. The greatest force behind our dominance as a species is the result of our ability to solve problems. The downfall for our species is that we have identified with our minds. We believe that who we are is our minds and bodies.

Our sense of separation, resulting from our identification with our mind and body, has caused us to act out of fear, the fear of scarcity and the fear of loss. It is from this perspective that all our challenges arise from, be they at the individual or collective level. Further, it limits our potential to experience higher levels of consciousness and awareness.

Imagine an actor who is performing in a play. This actor has deeply identified with her character and is flawless in how she presents her character to the audience. When the play is over, she removes her make-up, changes her clothes, and goes home. The actor no longer plays the role of her character. She is now becoming a spouse, a parent, a friend, or a daughter. She may party with her friends, go camping, or go out on a date. What the actor can do off stage is endless.

When we identify with the mind or body, we are like the actor who still believes that she is her character when the play is over. We need to learn how to transcend our minds and experience the deeper and more profound aspects of ourselves. One of the most powerful tools for this purpose is meditation. The heart of meditation is returning to silence. It perceives the illusions of reality, and it connects us with the non-phenomenal realm.

Daily Exercise:

There are some key points to keep in mind when learning how to meditate:

1. Maintain an attitude of total acceptance and non-judgment for everything you experience.
2. Do not try to control, change, or resist anything that you experience.
3. Allow all that you experience the complete freedom to express itself.

4. When meditating, you may experience thoughts such as:
   a. My thoughts keep coming; they are not slowing down.
   b. This is too difficult.
   c. This is boring.
   d. I have more important things to do.
   e. This is not working.
   f. Am I doing this right?

Ignore these thoughts and continue to focus on the meditation.

Finally, there is no correct way or incorrect way to meditate as long as you are allowing yourself to be a witness to all of your experiences.

1. Sit down in a comfortable position, close your eyes, and breathe normally.
2. Place your attention on your breath by focusing on the sensations of it traveling in and out of your body.
3. As your focus on your breath, you will experience the appearance of thoughts. When they appear, simply ignore them and return your attention back to your breath.
4. If you keep your focus on your breath, there will come the point when you can maintain your awareness of it without any effort. When you

reach this stage, allow yourself to be the witness to all that appears in your awareness.

5. Notice how thoughts, sensations, and perceptions appear in your awareness and then fade away. These mental phenomena appear and disappear in your awareness. However, that which is awareness remains constant and unchanging.
6. The mental phenomena that you experience will have the qualities of being positive, neutral, or negative; yet, awareness itself is untouched by any of these qualities.
7. As you give less importance to the experiencing of mental phenomena, they will lose their energy, and your mind will become calm; you may even experience periods of stillness and space. If you do, know that stillness and space is also a mental phenomenon. Do not become attached to any experience; rather, remain as a witness to it.
8. Continue to meditate for as long as you desire.

Day 6
~
The Nature of Experience

Because we identify with our minds and bodies, we experience ourselves as being a separate and unique entity that exists in a world of other entities, both living and non-living. As I sit and write this passage, I am aware of the words that appear on the screen of my laptop. I am also aware of the room that I am in, my wife who is upstairs, and my dog that is lying on the carpet. I am aware of the song that is playing on the radio, and I am aware of myself. Because I experience thoughts and the sensations of my body, I believe that the words, the room that I am in, my wife, my dog, and the song are separate entities that exist outside of me. All these other entities are what are commonly known as "experience."

As we explored in the first section of this chapter, it is impossible to separate the awareness of an experience with the experience itself.

I offer you another exercise so that what I speak of can be directly experienced by you. Direct experience is vital when exploring the metaphysical. Without direct experience, all that we are left with is theory.

Daily Exercise:

This next exercise builds on the exercise from day 1 and will challenge your further in questioning how you perceive reality.

1. Sit in a comfortable place and close your eye, allow yourself to relax.
2. Breathing normally, place your focus on the flow of your breath. Notice the sensations that you experience as your breath flows in and out of your body.
3. Should you become distracted by thought, simply return your focus to your breath.
4. As you focus on your breath, do not judge any experience that you encounter. Welcome every experience that you have without making any attempts to change or modify it.
5. As you focus on your breath, do not hold any expectations of what should be happening. Do not exert any effort. Allow everything that happens to occur.
6. When you feel calm and relaxed, remove your focus from your breath and place it on your thoughts.
7. Notice that you are aware of your thoughts. As you focus on your thoughts, what happens to them? Do your thoughts change in any way? Do they change in their intensity? Do they seem to appear

and fade with time? Where do your thoughts arise from? Where do they go when they fade?
8. Now shift your attention from your thoughts to the sensations that you experience in your body.
9. Notice that you are aware of your sensations. As you focus on your sensations, what happens to them? Do your sensations change in any way? Do they change in their intensity? Do they seem to appear and fade with time? Where do your sensations arise from? Where do they go when they fade?
10. With your eyes closed, reach out and touch something. It could be the object that you are sitting on, your arm or leg, or an object in the room.
11. When you touch the object, ask yourself if you are experiencing the object itself or are experiencing the sensation of the object. Can you separate the sensation of the object from the object itself? Where does this sensation appear from? Where does this sensation go when it fades? Determine the answers to these questions for yourself.
12. Notice that you are aware of the changing of sensation as it comes and goes.
13. Now ask yourself if you can separate the awareness of sensation from the sensation itself.
14. Now open your eyes and look at an object. As you observe the object, ask yourself if you can separate the seeing of the object from seeing itself.

Determine the answer to this question for yourself.
15. Ask yourself if you can separate the awareness of seeing from the seeing itself.
16. Close your eyes again, and allow yourself to relax. When you are feeling relaxed, ask yourself is it possible to experience anything without the awareness of it. Determine the answer to this question for yourself.
17. Now ask yourself if it is possible to separate the awareness of experience from experience itself.

I hope that you will discover that awareness and experience are one in the same. This is because experience arises from awareness, also known as consciousness. What we refer to as experience is the phenomenal expression of consciousness, which is non-phenomenal. When this is understood, you will know intuitively that any sense of separateness is just an illusion that is created by the conceptual mind. From higher perspectives of consciousness, everything is one.

The reason that you were unable to determine the place where thoughts and sensations arise and fade is that they arise and fade from consciousness. The objects that you touched or saw also came from consciousness. Even your sense of existing, of being alive, is an expression of consciousness. Your sense of being aware arises from consciousness. That who you believe to be arises from consciousness.

There is a reason why you experience yourself as having a physical body, and that reason is that having a physical allows you to experience the phenomenal world. It was stated earlier in this book that the fundamental aspect of the universe is energy and energy that is aware. That energy is consciousness and consciousness is constantly expanding through the gaining of information. Information can only be gained through experience. Since consciousness is non-phenomenal, it cannot experience anything other than itself. In other words, awareness can only know awareness. To gain information it needs to manifest as phenomenal objects (like you and me) so that it can have an experience. It is through experience that information is gained.

Whenever you have an experience, you are informing the pure consciousness (from which you manifested from) of that experience through the information that you gained from it. The information which we gain from experience is thought.

Thought provides consciousness with information that it can use to expand and create new manifestations, which are consistent with the information that it received. What is commonly known as the Law of Attraction is this process that the pure consciousness is constantly performing.

Day 7
~
The Psychological Self

The idea that we are phenomenal expressions of a larger consciousness can be difficult to comprehend because we experience the world at a conceptual level. It requires the transcendence of our normal consciousness awareness for this idea to become self-evident. Luckily, most of us experience this transcendence when we go to bed at night.

When you dream at night, you take on an altered state of consciousness. In the unfolding of your dream, you experience yourself in the dream as your dream self. Your dream self has thoughts, feelings, and perceptions of the dream world that it finds itself in. It can make decision, plan, anticipate, and take action as it engages with its dream world. As real as your dream may seem, while it is occurring, both your dream self and its dream world are the projections of your sleeping self. Similarly, your experience of being a separate and unique being, in your waking life, is also a projection of pure consciousness.

When we awake from a dream, it becomes evident to us that the dream self that we experienced was just a psychological manifestation of ourselves. The reason why our dream self, and its dream experience, was so real for us is that consciousness identified with it. The reason why consciousness identified with it was that our dream was based on thoughts that were meaningful to us. Similarly, you identify with your mind and body because the thoughts and beliefs that you hold of your mind and body are meaningful to you as well.

Your dream self is a psychological self that you experience while sleeping just as your waking self is the psychological self that is the projection of the pure consciousness. There is, however, a stage of consciousness where we transcend our psychological self.

Unlike dream sleep, we are free of thought in a deep sleep. Deep sleep is pure consciousness. When we enter deep sleep, pure consciousness removes its awareness from the world of objects (which includes thoughts) and redirects its attention toward itself. In a deep sleep, awareness is observing awareness.

Because deep sleep is devoid of thought, we have no memory of it. To have a memory requires experience, which deep sleep is devoid of. When we wake up in the morning, we are aware that we experienced deep sleep, but we have no recollection of the experience of it. Further, in a deep sleep, we lose all experience of ourselves. The reason why we felt rejuvenated and vitalized after waking from deep sleep is that we forgot about our existence as a person. We forgot about our existence as a person because our essential self was reunited with itself.

Daily Exercise:

This next exercise involves self-inquiry as you explore the nature of that which you refer to as "you." When performing this exercise, it is critical that you do not rely on what you believe that you know. Instead, I want to rely purely on your direct experiences as you perform this exercise. Do not go by what you think; go by what you experience. Also, I recommend that you read through this meditation first before practicing it. Or, record it on audio tape and play it back as you do this exercise.

1. When answering this question, do not rely on your thinking. You will not get an answer.

2. Sit down in a comfortable position and close your eyes.

3. Allow yourself to follow your breath during inhalation and exhalation. Place your attention on your breath. Feel it as it courses through your body.

4. Take on an attitude of complete allowing, that whatever arises during this meditation you will have complete acceptance of it.

5. Observe the perceptions, thoughts, sensations, feelings, and emotions that arise within you. Allow them to come and go on their own accord. All you need to do is be the observer of them.

6. You are the observer of thought, sensation, perception, emotions, and feeling. You are the one that is aware of experience. But who are you? You refer to yourself as "I," but who is this "I"?

7. Where is this "I"? Can you find where this "I" is located? Is it located in your body? Is it located in your heart?

8. The word "phenomenal" means something that can be seen, thought of, touched, heard, or detected somehow.

9. As you search for the location of "I," know that whatever you encounter is phenomenal in nature.

10. Anything you experience is phenomenal, everything you know is phenomenal.

11. Even if you experience space, a sense of emptiness, or bliss, this is not who you are. Space, emptiness, and bliss are also phenomenal because they can be detected by you.

12. Are you phenomenal? Everything that is phenomenal is subject to change. Your thoughts, sensations, feelings, and emotions are constantly changing.

13. Your thoughts come in and out of awareness? Who is observing thought coming in and out of awareness? Are you coming in and out of awareness?

14. Your emotions and feelings are constantly changing? Are you constantly changing?

15. No matter what your response is to these questions, there is awareness of your response. What is aware of your response?

16. The essence of who you are does not change; it is eternal.

17. Who you are cannot be observed; it cannot be felt, and it cannot be detected. Who you are is not phenomenal.

18. Who you are cannot be experienced. Who you are is awareness itself. Just as a ray of light cannot shine on itself, the awareness that is you cannot observe itself. You have a knowing that you exist.

19. The more you discover that which you are not, the closer you will come to realizing who you are.

20. This is the end of this meditation. Allow yourself to remain in silence for as long as you desire.

Week 2
Γ
The Power of Thoughts and Beliefs: How the Mind creates Reality

If we use the analogy of a computer, thoughts are units of information just as bits are units of information for a computer. Because we identify with our minds and bodies, we believe that we are the creator's of thought, that the thoughts that we have belong to us. Just as your dream self appears to think during the course of the dream, your psychological self also appears to be thinking.

At the most fundamental level, everything is one. What we interpret to be "our thoughts" is really our manifested self attracting thoughts that are consistent with the level of consciousness that we have reached. Every living being is tapping into the collective consciousness and attracting the information that is consistent with its conscious awareness. Sometimes referred to as the Akashi Records, the collective consciousness contains every thought that has ever, or will ever, be thought.

The greater consciousness system refers to all aspects of consciousness. It includes pure consciousness, all manifestations of pure consciousness, and the localized consciousness that is experienced by each manifested expression of consciousness.

It is the nature of pure consciousness to seek expansion as well as to support the success and happiness of each of its manifestation. In carrying out these functions, the pure consciousness employs thought.

Thought is the information that is generated by experience, which informs all aspects of the greater consciousness system. Further, it is the informing of the various components of the larger consciousness system that leads to the expansion of consciousness, both of pure consciousness and that of its localized expressions. Here is an example of how this process works:

A child (a manifestation of consciousness that experiences localized consciousness) is trying to figure out how to solve a math problem. The child's attempts do not lead to the resolving of the problem. The child's attempts are guided by thought, the thought that he or she attracted.

 If the thoughts lead to actions that do not solve the desired outcome, an experience of contrast occurs. In this case, the contrast is the result of the desired outcome (the resolution of the problem) and what the child experiences, the problem remains unsolved. The experience of contrast leads to the greater consciousness to manifesting other phenomena that are consistent with the child's desired outcome. As a result, the child gains access to thoughts of how to solve the problem that it did not consider before. The child changes their approach to solving the problem until the problem is solved. The flow of information (thought) is what leads to the expansion of localized consciousness (the child) and that of pure consciousness.

Thought is the conceptual representation of consciousness's infinite potential for expression. Because of our conceptual mind, we are unable to experience the infinite potential of consciousness, so the thoughts that we attract are like a snapshot of that infinite intelligence. To better understand this, it is like comparing a single frame with the full-length movie that it came from. Most of us are at the conscious level where we can only detect a single frame. The higher the level of conscious awareness that we achieve the more of the movie we can experience.

The ultimate purpose of studying metaphysics is to apply the teachings to our lives so that we can expand our awareness. The greater the expansion of awareness, the closer we come to realizing the truth of our own existence.

While thoughts are bits of information, beliefs are those thoughts that we take to be true. Beliefs are those thoughts of which we have developed a great sense of certainty for. Referring back to the movie metaphor, holding onto a belief is like us seeing a single frame of the movie and believing to know the movie's plot.

Because of our sense of certainty in our beliefs, they determine our experience of life. Like tinted sunglasses, beliefs color our experience of the world and ourselves. If I believe that the world is a dangerous place, then that will be my experience of the world. If I believe love is the foundation of life that that will be my experience of life.

Like everything else that is phenomenal, thoughts arise from the non-phenomenal. Further, thoughts are a vital aspect of the manifestation process. The manifestation process occurs in stages and starts off with the manifestation of desire. Desire is the initial and most fundamental manifestation of pure consciousness. Desire then manifest as thought, which contains information that is consistent with desire. In turn, thought manifest as emotions. Emotions manifest into action, and action manifest as physical form. This process is so ingrained in us that we are not even aware of it. Further, we only pay attention to the final stage, which is the actual manifestation. Most of us are unaware of all the stages that lead up to the actual manifestation. Additionally, we take the credit or the blame for the final manifestation.

Imagine a person who faces an obstacle; they need to increase their income because they are unable to make ends meet. The manifestation of a solution to this person's obstacle is desire, the desire to earn more money. Desire than manifest as thought, the thought of what this person can do to change their situation. The thought this person attracts could be the thought of looking for a new job, thoughts of the kind of job that they want, or thoughts of how to manage their money more effectively, and so on.

The thoughts that this person attract then manifest into emotion. Emotion creates the energy to turn thoughts into action. The emotions that this person experiences could be the emotion of fear or frustration for their current situation, or it could be the emotion of passion to make a change in their fiancés. Either way, emotions provide the fuel for change. The pain of financial struggle makes the person want to make a change while passion drives them forward. Emotion then manifest as action: The person searches for employment opportunities, sends out resumes, and develops a budget. With continued focus, action turns into physical form, which may include a new job and more money.

Notice that through our socialization process, which causes us to identify with our mind and body, we put all of our focus on the action component. The actual manifestation, the new job, and more money were a product of all the previous steps. The final step, the step of action, is what activated the inherent power found in each of the previous steps.

Day 8
~
Values

This week is about transforming your thoughts and beliefs so that they support you by reducing the resistance that you experience within yourself. By reducing your resistance, you improve your alignment with pure consciousness. Day 8 is about identifying your values.

Values are an indicator of what we value in life. Unlike the way values are traditionally thought of, the values that I speak of have to do with states of being or emotional states that we value. For example, a common traditional value would that of family. For our discussion, family is not a value. However, the emotional states that having a family give us is a value. Examples of values include:

- Love
- Compassion
- Contribution
- Security
- Fun
- Transcendence

Anytime we live in a manner that is inconsistent with our values; we create major resistance in our lives. If your life is not aligned with your values, start the process of making changes in your life so that you can start creating greater alignment. If you currently have a job that conflicts with your values, what can you do to create the needed changes in your work? Could you conduct your work differently? Would it require you take on a different position? Perhaps it means finding a new job. If the relationship you are in does not align with your values, what changes do you need to make? Do you need to transform your relationship or find a new one? Take into account any aspect of your life where you experience a gap between the way you live your life and the values that you hold.

The following are examples of creating resistance by going against our values:

- You value passion but do not pursue your dreams out of fear losing the security of the job that you hate.
- You value connection but pending all your time working when rather than being with your family.
- You value personal growth but always do things the same way just because you were taught or raised to believe that it is the way that it should be done.

Daily Exercise:

Create a list of your values and order them according to how important they are to you. You can identify your values by asking the question "What is most important in my life?" Remember, you are going for states of emotion or feeling. If family or money is what is most important to you, determine the emotions or feelings that you believe that family or money would give you. For each value you identify, determine if the way you live your life conflicts with these values.

Here is an example:

1. What is most important in my life? My wife.
2. My values are those emotional states that I value. Because my wife offers me love and connection, my true values are love and connection.
3. I need to ask myself if there are ways that I live my life that conflict with desire for love and connection. Example: I get defensive when she is upset with me.

Day 9
~
Beliefs

In Day 8, you identified your values. Today, you will identify your core beliefs that may be conflicting with that which you value.

Ultimately, the resistance that we experience in our lives is due to the conflicting beliefs that we hold. Frequently, just by identifying the belief that is generating resistance will automatically lead to that belief losing its potency. The following exercise is for identifying the beliefs behind your resistance.

Daily Exercise:

Make a list of the situations in your life that are causing you conflict or making you frustrated. When writing your items for your list, expand upon them so that you have a clear understanding of what is involved. Example: Instead of listing your spouse, write "When my spouse criticizes me." You will use this list in the exercise for day 10.

Day 10
~
Accessing your beliefs

When you have completed your list, choose the item that is most important for you to address. When you have selected your item, I want you to rephrase your item by rewording it in the following manner: "What does it mean to me_____.I have provided an example of how to approach this exercise by using the problem "I feel angry because my boss is always criticizing me."

1. I reword my problem to read: "What does it mean to me to have my boss criticize me?"

2. I would then respond to that question by writing: "It means that he is unfair."

3. I would then ask myself, "What does it mean to me to that he is unfair?

4. I would respond by saying that "It means he does not appreciate me."

5. I would then ask "What does it mean to me that he does not appreciate me?"

6. I would respond "It means that I am not good enough."

7. I would then ask "What does it mean that I am not good enough?"

8. I would respond with "It means that I am not worthwhile."

You want to continue this line of thinking until you cannot go any further with your questioning.

At the surface level, I believe that I am angry with my boss's criticism. However, the root belief that is causing me problems is that I believe that I am not worthwhile. Because I do not recognize that is my root belief, I become reactive to my boss's behavior. If I truly believed that I was worthwhile, I would find ways to deal with the situation that benefits me and hopefully my boss.

Day 11
~
Changing a Belief

In this section you will use the belief that you identified in Day 10 and transform it.

Transforming limiting thoughts

Once you have identified your root belief (from the previous exercise), you can change that belief by using the following exercise:

1. Get two sheets of paper. Select paper sizes of 8" x 11" or larger.

2. Take the first sheet of paper and fold it in half lengthwise.

3. On the top of the paper, write down your root belief.

4. Make a list on the left-hand side of the paper of all the ways this belief has cost you in your life. When doing this part of the exercise, think of how this root belief has affected you in all your life areas. Ask yourself how this belief has affected you in the way you see yourself, how it has affected your emotional health, your relationships, your

physical health, your work, your finances, and so on.

5. When writing, keep in mind the following:

    - When writing this list, write down the first thing that comes to your mind, even if it seems irrelevant.

    - Write as fast as you can and feel the emotions that arise. This is a heartfelt exercise, not a thinking one.

    - Keep writing until you run out of things to write.

6. By each item that you write down, assign an arbitrary point value as to how much impact this item has had on you. When selecting the point value, choose the first number that comes to mind.

7. When you have completed assigning the point values, find the total of all the point values and place it at the bottom of the page.

8. For the right side of the page, repeat Steps 6-7, except this time, you will write down all the ways that this belief has benefited you.

When you have completed Step 8, think of a new alternative belief that empowers you. For example, if the original belief was "No one will ever love me," my new belief maybe "The only love that I can depend on is the love that I give to myself."

On the second paper, repeat steps 1-8, using your new belief, with the following exceptions: Reverse Steps 6 and 8 by writing down all the ways that you believe that you would benefit from this new belief for Step 6. When doing Step 8, write down all the ways you believe it will cost you.

When you have completed the two sheets, do the following:

1. Immediately review your lists, allowing yourself to fully experience any emotions that arise.

2. Review your lists every day, once in the morning and once before you go to bed until you become fully associated with the emotions that you experience.

When you become fully associated with the costs for holding on to your old belief with the benefits of adopting your new belief, your mind will become programmed with your new belief.

Day 12
~
Preparing for Change

In this exercise, you will make list of actions that you can take that are consistent with your new empowering belief that you created in the last exercise. Here is an example:

- My old root belief was that "I am not worthy."
- My new belief (developed through the day 11 exercise) is "I am worthy just by the fact that I exist."

For today's exercise, I made a list all the actions that I could take to demonstrate that I am worthy. For example:

- Treat myself to a fancy dinner.
- Honor my feelings and spend the day doing only what I want to do.
- Go on that trip that I always wanted to take.

When your list is complete, I want you to schedule a time and date when you will commit to doing those actions that you have selected from your list.

Day 13 & 14
~
Acceptance and Resistance

Because we experience ourselves as having a mind and body, we experience ourselves as being separate from the rest of the world. Given that we experience ourselves as being separate, we resist those aspects of our experience that we find painful, such as certain thoughts or sensations.

Someone who had a bad relationship may resist experiencing thoughts of that relationship or the sensations (feelings and emotions) of their lingering pain. When we resist our thoughts and sensations, we cut ourselves off from the deeper aspects of us. We cut ourselves off from our connection with pure consciousness by identifying with the thoughts and sensations that we are avoiding. If we did not identify with our painful thoughts and sensations, we would not resist them, allowing us to focus on silence and the nature of awareness.

The power of acceptance is that it allows us to release our resistance and our identification to that which we are resisting. I stated earlier that we attract those thoughts that are consistent with our sense of self. If we are resisting any aspect of ourselves, what that we really doing is placing our focus on that which we do not want. We cannot resist anything without being vigilant of it.

By learning to accept our experiences, we reduce our attachment to them. When I speak about acceptance, it does not mean going against how we feel about a situation and pretend that it does not matter. Rather, acceptance means acknowledging the existence of the situation and not fighting against it. Once we accept a situation, we can place our focus on that which we desire.

One of the ways we create resistance in our lives is to go against those things that we value for our lives. If I value love and connection but become defensive, when I feel vulnerable, I am being resistant to that which I value. The following exercise will help you identify those areas in your life where there is a conflict in your values.

Daily Exercise:

Another way we create resistance within ourselves is to agree to do things, which go against how we genuinely feel. This next exercise addresses this.

Schedule a day where you will commit to doing only those things that you feel good about. This exercise is difficult for many people because we are so conditioned to being responsible by our parents and society. We believe that to have self-worth we need to be responsible and meet the expectations of others. If you have trouble with this exercise, doing it for less than a day and gradually increase the period of time till you can do it for a full day.

You may be thinking that this exercise is unrealistic. After all, there are things that we all have to do which we rather avoid. The focus of this exercise has less to do with the task at hand and more about the resistance that we are experiencing. Should there be something that requires your attention, of which you are experiencing resistance, your goal is to lower your resistance before you engage in that task. The following are steps for lowering your resistance.

1. Think about the benefits of doing the task and the consequences of not doing it. If the benefits of completing the tasks outweigh the consequences of not doing it, you should feel less resistance doing the task.
2. Think of how you could change your approach to doing the tasks in a manner that makes doing it more enjoyable. Example: If you need to pull weeds from your garden, listen to your favorite music as you are weeding.
3. If none of the previous suggestions change the way you feel about the task, postpone doing the task until you come to point where you can do it with acceptance.

Week 3
Θ
Focus: The Mind's Sword for cutting through Obstacles

In the last two chapters, we have covered the nature of silence, of consciousness, of experience, and of thoughts and beliefs. With the exception of experience, most of us associate these topics with the mind. In many teachings of meditation, we are told that the goal is to achieve a "silent mind." We also believe that consciousness, thoughts, and beliefs are contained in the mind.

As for the mind, many spiritual teachings make out the mind to be our enemy, that it impedes the attainment of enlightenment.

We are far enough into this book that I feel ready to expose another illusion that most of us have bought into. There is no mind. The mind does not exist. The mind is just another concept that we have created. Just as you have a psychological self, you also have a "mind" that the psychological self believes in. Both your psychological self and your mind are thoughts that we, as a species, have believed into existence.

That most of the human race has a conviction that they are a physical body with a mind is a testament to the power of beliefs. That which we believe becomes our reality and the belief in the existence of a mind is no different. What we believe to be a mind is the attraction of thoughts to our most fundamental thought, the psychological self.

Because of our deep-seated conviction of having a mind, it is easier to work with the mind to transcend it than it is to go fight against it. As we reach higher levels of awareness, it will eventually become self-evident that neither our minds nor our psychological selves are real. We learn to accept their existence, as illusionary aspects, without becoming attached to or personalizing them. Like anything else that we experience, the mind is just another object in awareness, which is our essential self.

The power of our minds is infinite, though the mind itself is illusionary. It is infinite it is power because it is a projection of consciousness that mirrors the infinite potential of consciousness. When we personalize our mind by believing that it is who we are, we are like the servant who unquestionably serves their master. When you create distance between you and your mind and can observe it, then you are moving in the direction where your mind becomes the servant of you.

The ability to become the masters of our own minds, and transcend to higher levels of consciousness, is purely the function of our ability to control our focus. The ability to control our focus is the center of all teachings, be they metaphysical or not. Whether it is solving a math problem or transcending thought, it is our ability to direct our attention that makes it possible to expand consciousness. Ultimately, it is the redirecting of attention away from objects and toward awareness itself that leads to true freedom. For this book, I define true freedom as the ability to transcend the perceived limitations that are imposed by the identification with the mind and body.

In the following days of this week, you will learn ways that you can use your focus to improve the quality of your life by transcending the sense of limitation that is imposed by our belief in the mind.

Day 15
~
Problem Solving

Albert Einstein once said, "No problem can be solved from the same level of consciousness that created it." All problems that we experience are a result of our own thinking. The flaw in our thinking that leads to humanity's problems is that we see ourselves as being separate from others. Because everything in life is interconnected, we create problems when we ignore the interconnectedness of life.

Our inability to perceive the interconnectedness of life is not limited to our relationships with those around us. It also extends to our inability to perceive our interconnectedness with our essential selves. Because of this ignorance, we find ourselves being swayed by our limited beliefs. Examples of such beliefs include:

- "It can't be done."
- "That idea is impossible."
- "I need to be realistic."
- "I will never figure this out."
- "It is too hard."
- "I have tried everything."
- "This always happens to me."
- "I am not smart enough."
- "I can't figure it out."
- "I give up."

As stated earlier, the thoughts that we hold attract other thoughts of like kind. One way to practice problem-solving from higher levels of consciousness is through the use of intention and silence. There are basic steps to problem-solving from higher levels of awareness:

- Silence
- Intention
- Detachment

Silence: We can achieve a state of mental calm by going into meditation, being out in nature, physical exercise, or whatever works for you. However you reach it, you want to enter a state where you are feeling calm yet alert. Of all the ways to do this, the practice of meditation is most effective.

Intention: When you have reached the state of mental calm, express your intention to yourself with a sense of certainty. It is important that you believe that your intention is possible. If you harbor doubt, that is what will be communicated to the larger consciousness system. Examples of intentions would be:

- I have the job that I desire.
- I am healing my relationship.
- I am becoming stronger.
- I am overcoming this challenge.
- The solution to my problem will appear when the time is right.
- The solution to my problem exists already; I just need to be ready to receive it.

- I am enjoying the process of discovering the solution to my problem.
- It feels good to know that I am learning to access higher levels of awareness for problem solving.

Notice that these examples are not all directed at achieving the final answer to the problem. Some of these intentions are process oriented rather than results oriented. If you find yourself harboring any doubts of achieving your intention, go with a process-oriented intention.

Example:

- Outcome-oriented: I am healing my relationship.
- Process oriented: I am enjoying learning about my relationship.

Whether your intentions are process oriented or results oriented does not matter, both will get you to your answer when the time is right for you to receive the answer.

When formulating your intentions, observe the following criteria:

- They must be sincere and heartfelt.
- The outcome of your intentions needs to benefit all those who are impacted by your intentions.
- They need to be stated in the positive.
- They need to be stated in the present tense.

Detachment

Once you have communicated your intention, the next step is to practice detachment. Detachment means placing your focus on something that is unrelated to solving your problem. If you continue to focus on getting the answer to your problem, you will risk becoming disappointment or experience doubt. Since the vibrational level of your doubt or disappointment will be stronger than your trust in the manifestation process, your answer will remain elusive. The best formula for detachment is to become silent, release your intention, and get on with your life!

Daily Exercise:

Make a list of intentions that you have which would be meaningful you, if you could make them your reality. Be sure to craft them as described in this section. You will use your list in Day 16.

Day 16

~

Manifestation

For the rest of this week, practice the manifestation process using your list from Day 15. Follow the steps that you learned in Day 15:

1. Become silent (using meditation is recommended).
2. Express your intention silently to yourself.
3. Practice detachment.

When doing this exercise, do not get involved in the outcome that you experience. In other words, do not get disappointed if your intentions do not manifest right away. In the beginning, just focus on the process. Your intentions will manifest as you learn to develop your sense of acceptance for whatever appears in your life.

Day 17 & 18
~
Visualizations

Visualizing is great for accessing and influencing the subconscious. Visualization is also a valuable tool for turning your intentions into reality. However, there are aspects of the visualizing process that are often misunderstood. The following are some key points to consider when visualizing:

1. There is an abundance of visualizing programs available on the market, and they can be useful if you have never visualized before. However, the most effective visualizations occur when you create your own visualizations. Once you understand the process, learn to trust your imagination and just go with it.
2. Many people feel they are unable to visualize, as they are unable to develop clear images in their mind. Do not worry about the quality of your images. However you experience your visualizations, trust them. Some people are unable to see images; rather, they experience sensations. With continued practice, your visualizations will become more vivid.
3. Before visualizing, it's helpful to formulate an intention for yourself. Examples of intentions would be:

a. Visualizing your desires already manifested
b. Visualizing yourself exploring that which you are resisting.
c. Visualizing you taking on a new challenge as a form of a mental rehearsal.
d. Visualizing you solving a problem.

Daily Exercise:

Practice incorporating the visualization process into this week's lesson of manifesting your intentions. **Note:** While you want to remain dethatched from your intentions, you still can visualize them. When we are attached to our intentions, we are thinking about how or when they will manifest. When we visualize our intentions, we are focusing on the intention itself, not how or when it will occur.

Day 19
~
Changing Perception

Most of us experience the world through our perspective of life. The ability to step into the perspective of another is a powerful tool for creating empathy and understanding with the people in our life.

1. Think about the person whose perspective you want to enter.
2. When thinking about this person, think of their frustrations and concerns that they have and the reasons for it. You do not have to understand or even agree with their perspective; your job is to just recognize their frustrations.
3. Announce to yourself your intention to enter this person's perspective.
4. Enter your meditation, reminding yourself again of your intention.
5. When you reach a calm mental state, repeat the intention one last time. From this point on, do make any attempts to influence your experience or hold any expectations. Simply remain open and allow whatever you experience to present itself.
6. Practice by repeating this exercise until you experience the perceptive of the other person.

Like most of the exercises provided in this book, this exercise takes practice. Do not get disappointed if this exercise did not work for you. It takes time to recondition our minds to successfully to this exercise. When you can get this exercise to work for you, try it out with animals!

Week 4
Φ
Feelings and Emotions: Messengers from the Universe

Our feelings and emotions play a major role the development of higher levels of awareness by providing us with feedback to our alignment with our essential self. You and I are multidimensional beings in that we are both non-phenomenal and phenomenal. Our essential self is non-phenomenal while our manifested form is phenomenal. What is referred to as "enlightenment" is when our phenomenal self becomes aligned with our non-phenomenal self.

What cause us to get out of alignment are the thoughts and beliefs that we identify with. There are two stages of the alignment process. The first stage is alignment that results from focusing on those thoughts that empower and support us in our happiness. The second stage is when we transcend all thoughts and focus on awareness itself. This section focuses largely on the first stage; many of Week 1's exercises addressed the second stage.

Emotions are the palpable expression of thoughts; they are a mirror to our thoughts. The quality of our emotions that we experience reflects the thoughts that we are placing our attention on. If you are angry it is because you are focusing on angry thoughts. If you are feeling peaceful, it is because you are focusing on peaceful thoughts. We can improve our alignment with pure consciousness by identifying those thoughts that are causing us unhappiness. Sometimes it is difficult to identify our thoughts that are causing us unhappiness, especially when those thoughts are subconscious. By noticing the quality of our emotions, we can readily identify the thoughts that are behind them.

Unlike our emotions, our feelings are not a reflection of thoughts. Rather, they are an indicator to our alignment with pure conscious. While our feelings are our primary indicator to our alignment, our emotions are a secondary indicator of alignment. Emotions only indicate the quality of our thoughts. I recommend that you read through these meditations first before practicing it. Or, record them on audio tape and play it back as you do this exercise.

Day 20
~
Observing Sensations

The sensations of the body, both pleasant and an unpleasant, inform us of whether we are in alignment with the highest aspect of ourselves. This exercise will help you become more aware of the sensations of your body.

1. Close your eyes and allow yourself to follow your breath during inhalation and exhalation. Place your attention on your breath. Feel it as it courses through your body.

2. Now place your attention on the sensations of the body. Place your attention on any sensation of the body that appears in your awareness.

3. Do you feel a tingling in your hands or feet? Do you feel tension in your back, shoulders, or face? Do you feel the weight of your body or the pressure on your buttocks from the chair or ground that you are sitting on?

4. Allow yourself to experience the sensations of the body without any judgment of any of them, even the ones that may feel unpleasant. Sensations are just that sensations, there are no good or bad sensations. Good and bad, pleasant and unpleasant, these are value judgments that exist solely in mind. The same thing is true with perceptions, sounds, and thoughts; they just are.

5. Are the sensations that you experience stable? Are they always the same or do they change? Are they always there or do they come and go?

6. Just stay in the awareness of your body's sensation, allow yourself to experience them for as long as you desire.

7. This is the end of this meditation; feel free to allow yourself to continue to meditate on the body for as long as you wish.

Day 21
~
Observing Emotions

This next meditation is about observing your emotions. To observe your emotions is to be aware of them. You can transform your emotions by simply being aware of them as well inquiring about their qualities.

1. Sit down in a comfortable position and close your eyes.

2. Allow yourself to follow your breath during inhalation and exhalation. Place your attention on your breath. Feel it as it courses through your body.

3. Have complete acceptance for whatever you experience during this meditation.
4. Observe the perceptions, thoughts, sensations, feelings, and emotions that arise within you. Allow them to come and go on their own accord. All you need to do is be the observer of them.

5. Now pay attention to any emotion that arises. Become an observer of it, what happens when your focus is placed on your emotion?

6. Do not place any meaning on the emotion you experience; do not think of it as being positive or negative. Words such as "positive", "negative," "pleasant," or "unpleasant" are products of the mind

7. There is no intrinsic meaning to anything in life. All meaning is derived from our minds. Emotions and feelings have no power of their own; they derive all their power from the attention we give them.

8. When observing emotions, do so with complete allowing; do not try to change anything about it.

9. As you observe your emotions, do you notice a change in how you experience them? Do they change in intensity? Do they become stronger or milder? Can you locate where they come from? Can you observe where they go?

10. As you observe emotions, ask yourself "Am I my emotions or am I the one that is aware of them?" If a feeling or emotion is experienced as being unpleasant, does awareness feel unpleasant? If an emotion is experienced as being pleasant, does awareness feel this pleasant?

11. Awareness does not experience anything; awareness only elucidates experience. Awareness is like a beam of light shining on a snow-covered field. The light does not feel the cold of the snow; it only illuminates it. As you observe emotions, be as the beam of light.

12. This is the end of this meditation. Feel free to remain in meditation for as long as you wish.

Day 22

~

Transforming Sensations

Using awareness, you can not only develop your powers of discernment but to also transform what you focus on. In this exercise, you will transform your experience of sensations.

1. Sit down and make yourself comfortable, if you like, you can close your eyes.
2. Place your attention on your breath as it travels in and out of your body. Allow your awareness to wash over your body and experience the sensations of the body.//
3. Now scan your body with your awareness for a relaxed, calm, or pleasant sensation. When you find such a sensation, allow yourself to focus on it.
4. As you observe this sensation, I want you to ask yourself the following question: "What color is this sensation?" Accept the first response that comes to mind.
5. Now ask "What size is this sensation?" Again, go with the first answer that comes to mind.

6. Now ask yourself "Does this sensation have a texture to it? Is it smooth, rough, soft, or hard?"

7. Now search the body for a sensation that is not relaxed, calm, or pleasant. Perhaps it has a tension, pressure, heaviness, or hardness to it.

8. Now just as with the pleasant sensation, ask yourself: "What are the color, size, and texture of this sensation?"

9. Now using your awareness, allow yourself to imagine that the qualities of the unpleasant sensation take on the qualities of the pleasant sensation. If the pleasant sensation had a green color, imagine the color of the unpleasant sensation changing to green. If the texture of the pleasant sensation was soft, imagine the unpleasant sensation grow soft, and so on.

10. Take your time as you transfer the qualities of the pleasant sensation to the unpleasant sensation.

11. Now observe the unpleasant sensation. Has the sensation changed? Has this sensation develop a more pleasant quality to it? If not, continue to practice this meditation.

12. This is the end of this meditation.

Day 23
~
Experience Freedom

Most instructions for meditation advise you to sit in a comfortable position while sitting straight in an upright position. One of keys to meditation is learning to be allowing of all experiences, to not control anything. The same is true with the body. In this meditation, you will listen to the body and allow it to move or position itself in complete freedom.

1. Sit down and make yourself comfortable and allow yourself to relax.

2. Close your eyes and focus on your breath, allow yourself to become relaxed.

3. Forget about what you learned from your mother about sitting straight. If your body feels like slumping over, let it. Allow your body to do whatever it wants.

4. Place your awareness on the body and its sensations. Let your awareness be soft, and do not get caught up in your thinking. Simply observe the sensations of the body and any messages that you are getting from the body.

5. This is the end of this meditation. Please feel free to allow yourself to listen to your body for as long as you desire.

Day 24

~

Trust your Feelings

Our feelings are informing us to whether we are moving toward or away from our own integrity as a human being. When we do not trust our feelings, we are unable to trust ourselves. This next meditation will involve noting how feelings and sensations are affected by our focus.

1. Sit down, close your eyes, and relax.
2. Allow yourself to become silent and observe the thoughts, feelings, emotions, and sensations that arise within. Allow all of these phenomena to present themselves to your awareness.

3. I want you to think of a situation that is currently causing you feelings of uneasiness, concern, or hurt. When you identify such a situation, allow yourself to focus on it. Relive the experience in your mind.

4. As you focus on the situation, become aware of the feelings that arise. Allow the feelings to arise naturally. Remember, your feelings are like a compass; they have a message for you. They are telling you to move toward or away from that

which you are focusing on. When we are making decisions, taking actions, or focusing on things that bring about pleasant feelings, we know that we are on the right track and are being consistent with our sense of integrity. Conversely, when we have feelings that are unpleasant, we are experiencing situations that are inconsistent with our sense of integrity.

5. Now ask yourself: "What can I do, believe, or focus on that will make me feel better about this situation?" Is there a decision that you need to make? Do you need let go of something? Do you need to question your thinking? Do you need to take time for yourself? Do you need to risk disappointing others?

6. Keep inquiring with yourself until you have identified a way to address the situation that leaves you feeling a sense of relief, calm, or peace.

7. When you come up with a solution to the situation that feels good to you, trust that this is the correct decision for you. Your feelings are completely accurate and reliable, for you, at this moment of time. If your feelings regarding your solution or the situation change, honor them as well.

8. Be sure not to confuse your feelings for your thoughts or beliefs. Your feelings are reliable; however, your thoughts and beliefs are not.

9. If you are unable to find a way to make yourself feel better, this is okay also. Allow yourself to remain with the feeling. Offer your feeling your full acceptance. Accepting our feelings and being at peace with them is an act of self- love and an indication of integrity.

10. This is the end of the meditation. Please remain in your stillness for as long as you like.

Day 25
~
Transforming Emotions

This next exercise will involve you playing a more active role than in the previous exercise, and it is a powerful tool if you have a strong negative emotion that has been lingering in you. I recommend that you read through this meditation first before practicing it. Or, record it on audio tape and play it back as you do this exercise.

Do the following:
1. Sit down and make yourself comfortable.
2. Close your eyes and allow yourself to relax
3. Place your attention on your breath as it enters and exits your body, focusing on the sensations you experience as you inhale and exhale.
4. If you are not already experiencing a negative emotion, relive a memory that will activate one. Think of a negative experience from the past or that you are currently experiencing.
5. When the unpleasant emotion arises, identify the emotion. Examples could be anger, fear, concern, sadness, etc.
6. When you have identified the emotion, describe what the emotion feels like. Notice: You want to describe what the emotion feels like, not what you think about it. To avoid falling into this trap, phrase your response as "It feels like_____?

Here are some examples:
- "It feels like it is crushing me."
- "I feel like I want to run away."
- "It leaves me feeling numb."
- "It feels like a boulder crushing me."

1. After you identify what the emotion feels like, repeat this process with the response that you give. Example:
    a. If the emotion that I am feeling is anger, my response to what it feels like is "It feels like my body is tightening."
    b. I would then repeat the process by asking "What does the tightening of the body feel like?
    c. My response to that could be "It feels like my body is hard."
    d. I would follow up with "What does a hard body feel like?"
    e. With every response that I give, I would repeat the same line of questioning until the emotion transforms into a positive emotion.

When describing the feeling of the emotion, go by the first answer that comes to you. Do not worry about getting it wrong; you can't. As long as you describe the feeling of the emotion without getting intellectual about it, you will be on the right track. Every time you describe an emotion, you allow it to transform itself. By continuously describing it every time that it transforms, the emotion will eventually transform into a positive emotion. Using this process facilitates the emotion to go full circle and heal itself.

Day 26
~
Letting go

There is nothing in your experience that does not arise from within you. We experience the world through perception, sensation, sound, and taste, all of which come from within us. These phenomena simply arise and fade within the space of your awareness on their own accord. So what are you holding onto? What are you trying to control? In this next meditation is about allowing.

1. Sit down and make yourself comfortable, allow yourself to relax. If you would like, you may close your eyes for now.

2. Allow yourself to relax as you focus on your breath, place your attention on your breath as it enters your body, travels through your body, and then leaves it as you exhale.

3. Breathe normally, without exerting any effort. Relax.

4. Allow yourself to develop a sense of total acceptance. Be totaling allowing of what appears in your awareness.

5. Do not judge, evaluate, or analyze anything that you experience.

6. Do not hold any expectations for what you should be experiencing.

7. Do not search for anything. Do not imagine anything. Do not create anything. Simply observe.

8. If unpleasant or uncomfortable thoughts, feelings, or sensation arise, let them be.

9. Allow all of your experiences to come into your awareness. Do not try to change them. Do not try to replace them with something that is more pleasant or positive.

10. You cannot do anything wrong. What you ever you are experiencing, this is the right experience for you.

11. Simply allow experience to flow through your awareness. Simply observe.

12. There is nothing for you to do. There is nothing for you to change. There is nothing for you to believe. Simply be the observer of all that presents itself.

13. This is the end of this meditation. Allow yourself to remain in silence for as long as you desire.

Day 27
Ω
Challenging Minds and Cultivating Freedom

If you have gone through all the exercises in the previous chapters, congratulations! It shows that you are committed to changing your experience of life and that you are open to new ideas. You may have found the contents in this book difficult to understand. If so, I recommend that you re-read it and repeat the exercises until they start to resonate with you. You do not have to understand everything in this book. Nor do you have to feel successful in all the exercises in order to get the full benefit of this book. When you revisit this book, which I hope you do, I would like you to consider some important points.

- Everything that has been written in this book is something that you do already know. The only difference between our everyday experience and what is described in this book is that our everyday experience is usually attributed to a function of the world around us or a function from within us. If I am caught in a traffic-jam and feel frustrated, I would attribute the situation to all the other drivers on the road and the building frustration that I am feeling. Because I experience myself as a separate entity, I see myself as a victim of my circumstances. After all, my experience of the being caught in traffic is the result of something outside myself, something that I cannot control. The fact that I feel frustrated should be no surprise.

The perspective I am tried to demonstrate to you through this book points to a drastically different understanding. The traffic jam, my experience of myself, my thoughts, perceptions, and sensation, are all objects within the field of awareness. Awareness takes in every possible experience that I could have. The truth of who I am is that awareness. Everything that has been written in this book is pointing to this.

If this perspective seems too extreme that is okay. If any aspect of this book resonates with you, it is my hope you will continue with this exploration. You and I have been operating under the conditioning of society from the time we were born. In turn, all the preceding generations were similarly indoctrinated.

There is nothing wrong with our experience of this world, or the experience we have of ourselves. Our challenge is when we limit ourselves to this perspective and remain unaware of our true potential, which is infinite. The truth of who you are is beyond what your mind can grasp!

- For the reasons just stated, your exercises for the rest of this day is to practice those exercises in this

book which feel right for you and review any part of this book that you may remain unclear about. Unless you had an understanding of metaphysics before reading this book, you will most likely have to reread it as there was a lot of information provided.
- Finally, I would like to leave you with one final point. From the introduction, there was the story of the farmer who was looking at the moon. You do not want to confuse the content of this book for what you are really seeking, which is expanded awareness. That which you ultimately desire exists within you already, and it always will. This book is just my way of pointing to it.

The End

Dear reader,

Before you close this book, I want to leave you with one last advice.

You should treat these four weeks as an introduction to the nature of consciousness. Your next step is to take those exercise that you practiced and make them a part of your daily lifestyle. Practice them and apply them whenever you can as you go through your day.

Finally, if you enjoyed the Power of Metaphysics then I´d like to ask you for a favor to leave an honest review on amazon. It´d be greatly appreciated.

Just type in this link to leave a review on amazon:

https://www.amazon.com/dp/B0776DS7W4

Thank you and good luck!

Erik